GRIEF IS A TEAM SPORT

Workbook

By

DR. FRED BATTEN, JR.

Watersprings
PUBLISHING

Published by Watersprings Publishing,

a division of Watersprings Media House, LLC.

P.O. Box 1284 Olive Branch, MS 38654

www.waterspringspublishing.com

Contact the publisher for bulk orders and permission requests.

Printed in the United States of America.

ISBN-13: **978-1-964972-16-9**

How to Use This Companion Journal

Welcome to your *Grief is a Team Sport* Companion Journal. This journal was created to walk alongside you as you read each chapter, giving you space to process, reflect, and engage with your grief journey in a deeper way.

Each chapter of this journal is designed to:

✔ Guide your reflections with prompts connected to the reading

✔ Ground your journey with scripture, quotes, and prayers

✔ Encourage active processing through fill-in-the-blank activities and personal definitions

✔ Help you apply insights from real-life stories to your own life

Here's how to use it:

1. Read each chapter in the main book first to understand the concepts and stories shared.

2. Pause with the journal. Take time with the reflection prompts. Write honestly—there are no right or wrong answers here.

3. Complete the activities to help you explore grief from different angles and prepare for healing.

4. Pray through the prayer prompts and write your own heartfelt prayers to God.

5. Return as needed. Grief isn't linear. You can revisit any page, reflection, or prayer as you navigate this journey.

Remember, grief is not a solo sport. Let this journal be your safe space to process your pain, recognize your team, and lean into the healing God offers.

CONTENTS

GRIEF, LIKE FOOTBALL,
REQUIRES THE RIGHT
FORMATION TO MOVE
FORWARD.

Chapter 1:

WHAT IS GRIEF, REALLY?

Objective:

To help you understand grief from multiple perspectives and begin identifying how it shows up in your life.

Key Scripture:

"The Lord is close to the brokenhearted and saves those who are crushed in spirit."
Psalm 34:18, NIV

What is Grief?

Grief is the natural, normal response to loss. It isn't just about death. Grief can be experienced through the loss of relationships, health, identity, jobs, safety, dreams, or seasons of life.

In the game of life, grief is the injury that stops the play—but healing is found when we return to the huddle, lean on our teammates, and reset the strategy.

Definitions from Leading Thinkers:

- **Elisabeth Kübler-Ross:** "Grief is the emotional response to loss, and it includes five stages: denial, anger, bargaining, depression, and acceptance."

- **David Kessler:** "Grief is not just about the person who died, but about the world that no longer exists."

- **Alan Wolfelt:** "Grief is what you think and feel on the inside after someone you love dies. Mourning is the outward expression of that grief."

- **Jamie Anderson:** "Grief is just love with nowhere to go."

Reflection Prompt:

Which of these definitions resonates with you the most? Why?

Types of Grief:

C_____ Grief

_____y Grief

Prolonged _____

C_____e Grief

Disenfranchised Grief

Real-Life Story:

When Darlene finally received healing after 25 years of struggle, there was immense joy. But there was also grief—grief for the years lost to pain, missed opportunities, and the emotional toll it took. Sometimes we grieve even when the outcome is good because we recognize what it cost us to get there.

Quote to Reflect On:

"Grief is love with nowhere to go." – Jamie Anderson

"Grief isn't the end of the game—it's halftime. It's where we regroup, refuel, and prepare to play again." – Grief is a Team Sport

Fill-in-the-Blank Activity:

1. To me, grief feels like _____.

2. The hardest part about my loss is _____.

3. When I think about what I've lost, I feel _____.

4. One thing I wish others understood about my grief is _____.

Activity: My Personal Definition of Grief

Grief is...

_____

_____

_____

_____

Prayer Prompt:

Dear God,

_____

_____

_____

_____

_____

Amen.

Closing Thought:

Grief is not a detour from your journey—it's part of the road. Understanding it is the first step in the healing process. And in this game of life, grief may sideline us, but healing happens when we stop trying to play solo.

In a culture that prizes strength and stoicism, grief is often mislabeled as a weakness. But expressing grief isn't a weakness, it's a witness.

Chapter 2

THE MYTHS WE'VE BEEN TOLD

Objective:

To challenge common misconceptions about grief that may block healing and create guilt, shame, or unrealistic expectations.

Key Scripture:

"Then you will know the truth, and the truth will set you free."
John 8:32, NIV

Real-Life Story:

Fred's friend lost her son and said, "People keep telling me to be strong, but I feel like breaking every day." The myth of strength being silent caused her to suffer alone. Once she realized she didn't have to hide her grief, she began to heal more authentically.

Top 5 Myths About Grief (And the Truths That Bust Them):

1. **Myth:** Grief follows stages in a neat order.
   Truth: Grief is messy. You may revisit stages multiple times or skip some entirely.

2. **Myth:** Time heals all wounds.
   Truth: Time alone doesn't heal. It's what you do with the time—processing, support, and self-care—that leads to healing.

3. **Myth:** If I cry, I'm weak.
   Truth: Tears are a healthy and holy part of grief. Even Jesus wept (John 11:35).

4. **Myth:** I should be over this by now.
   Truth: Grief has no expiration date. Your timeline is your own.

5. **Myth:** Moving on means forgetting.
    Truth: You never forget. You carry forward while honoring the past.

"Too many people try to be the MVP of grief, carrying it all alone. But healing comes when you pass the ball—when you let others in." – Grief is a Team Sport

Quote to Reflect On:

"Grief doesn't have a timeline, it has a rhythm—and some days the beat is heavy." – Unknown

Fill-in-the-Blank Activity:

- One myth I've believed about grief is _____ .

- That myth made me feel _____.

- I now choose to believe _____.

Activity: Truth Tellers

Make a list of truths that can replace harmful myths in your own experience.

(*Ex: "It's okay to miss them still." "Healing is not linear." "I can grieve and grow at the same time."*)

Prayer Prompt:

Dear God,

Replace the myths I've believed with Your truth. Teach me to walk in freedom, not false strength.

Amen.

Closing Thought:

Letting go of the myths frees you to grieve honestly—and healing begins in honesty. You're not disqualified because you hurt. You're still in the game.

Chapter 3:

YOUR GRIEF TEAM

Objective:

To help you identify the people, tools, and supports you need to navigate grief—because healing isn't a solo sport.

Key Scripture:

"Two are better than one… If either of them falls down, one can help the other up."
Ecclesiastes 4:9a-10, NIV

Real-Life Story:

During the hardest season of Fred's life, it wasn't a single act of comfort that helped—it was a team: Denise's prayers, friends who called to listen, church members who dropped off meals, and a counselor who offered a safe space to fall apart. Healing happened in the huddle.

Who's on Your Grief Team?

Your team may include:

- **Lifter -positive voice when you are struggling**
- **Listener – Someone who will sit and listen**
- **Weepers – allows you space for sorrow**
- **Supporters - Practical Helpers – bring meals, help with tasks**
- **You**

"Even the greatest athletes need a team around them. Grief recovery isn't a solo championship—it's a team effort every time." – Grief is a Team Sport

Activity: Build Your Grief Roster

Name your "Grief Team" like a sports roster. Include names, roles, and how they help you.

1. Someone I trust to support me emotionally is _____.

2. A spiritual voice I can turn to is _____.

3. A safe space I can go to when I'm overwhelmed is _____.

4. One person I will reach out to this week is _____.

Prayer Prompt:

Dear God,

Thank You for reminding me I don't have to grieve alone. Help me identify my team and give me the courage to reach out when I need support. Amen.

Closing Thought:

No one wins alone. Even Jesus, in His sorrow, called His disciples to watch and pray with Him. You're not weak for needing a team—you're wise.

Grief is a team sport. You weren't meant to do this alone. Healing happens best in a healthy community.

Chapter 4:

THE SPIRITUAL SIDE OF GRIEF

Objective:

To help you explore how grief affects your faith and how your spiritual foundation can serve as a source of healing and strength.

Key Scripture:

"Even though I walk through the darkest valley, I will fear no evil, for You are with me."
Psalm 23:4, NIV

Quote to Reflect On:

"God is not offended by your grief. He meets you in it." – Unknown

Real-Life Story:

During a personal season of deep loss, Jimmy found himself asking hard spiritual questions: "Why now?" "Why me?" "Where is God in this?" But the deeper the questions, the more he found that God could handle the weight of them. Faith didn't eliminate the grief—but it gave him a place to anchor when everything else felt like sinking sand.

Spiritual Responses to Grief:

Like teammates huddled before a big play, grief often leads us to spiritual reflection. Some people:

- **Run toward God** for comfort and strength.

- **Wrestle with God** like Jacob at the river.

- **Pull away** due to unanswered prayers or spiritual fatigue.

- **Find renewed purpose** through loss.

"Faith is not the absence of grief; it's the assurance that you're not alone in the locker room of loss." – Grief is a Team Sport

Reflection Questions:

1. How has your faith been affected by your grief?

_____

_____

_____

_____

2. Are you drawing closer to God, pulling away, or unsure where you stand?

_____

_____

_____

3. What do you believe God wants to say to you in your grief?

_____

_____

_____

_____

Spiritual Exercises:

- **Scripture Meditation:** Read and reflect on Psalm 34:18 and Romans 8:26-28.

- **Journaling Prompt:**
  "God, I don't understand _____, but I'm choosing to trust You with _____."

Activity: My Valley Prayer

Write a prayer or psalm expressing how you feel in your grief.

Dear God,

_____

_____

_____

_____

_____

_____

_____

_____

_____

_____

_____

_____

_____

Closing Thought:

Spiritual grief doesn't mean you've lost your faith—it means you're bringing your whole heart to God. Every team has timeouts. Let this be your spiritual timeout to regroup, breathe, and trust again.

You don't have to pretend with God. He walks with you through the valley—and leads you toward healing.

CHRISTIAN GRIEF,
THEN, IS NOT SILENT OR
SOLITARY.

Chapter 5:

The Faces of Grief - Emotional Impact

Objective:

To name and normalize the many emotions you may experience in grief—and give you a game plan for working through them.

Key Scripture:

"Jesus wept."

John 11:35, NIV

Real-Life Story:

After the loss of his brother, Fred cycled through waves of sadness, numbness, guilt, and even laughter. He learned that grief is not a one-emotion experience—it's a whole team of emotions taking the field at once.

The Emotional All-Star Team of Grief:

- **Sadness** – The most visible player.

- **Anger** – Sometimes aimed at God, others, or yourself.

- **Guilt** – "What could I have done differently?"

- **Fear** – "What's next?" or "Will this happen again?"

- **Numbness** – When feelings are too overwhelming to face.

- **Relief** – Especially after long suffering (which can bring guilt).

- **Laughter** – Yes, joy can show up in the huddle, too.

- **Loneliness**

- **Confusion**

"Grief is emotional overtime. There's no clock for how long it lasts—just the courage to keep showing up and playing through the pain." – Grief is a Team Sport

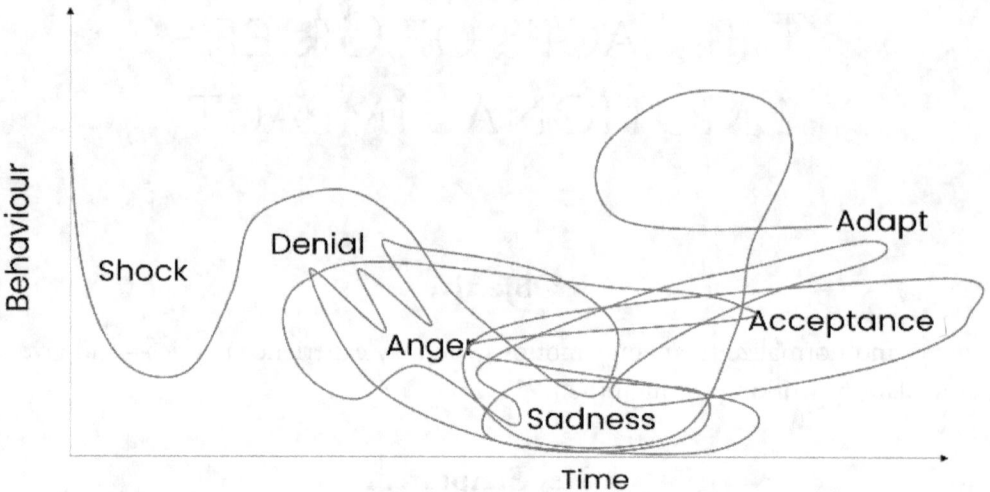

Source: richgoddard.co https://springhealth.com/blog/recognizing-grief-at-work/

Reflection Questions:

1. Which emotions have surprised you the most in your grief?

_____

_____

_____

_____

2. Have you judged yourself for feeling "too much" or "not enough"?

_____

_____

_____

_____

3. Which emotion is loudest for you right now?

_____

_____

_____

_____

Activity: Emotional Playbook

Write down five emotions you've felt in your grief. Next to each one, write a healthy way to process or express it (e.g., talking, crying, journaling, prayer, movement, counseling).

1._____

2._____

3._____

4._____

5._____

Prayer Prompt:

Dear God,

My emotions are all over the place. Thank You that I can bring them all to You. Teach me to feel, express, and heal—without shame. Amen.

Closing Thought:

Every emotion matters on the grief team. Some are loud. Some are quiet. But all are needed. Don't bench your feelings—let them speak, and then let God carry them.

Self-care isn't about escaping grief. It's about equipping yourself to survive it.

Chapter 6:

THE BODY KEEPS THE SCORE- PHYSICAL IMPACT OF GRIEF

Objective:

To identify how grief shows up in your body and encourage you to practice gentle self-care.

Key Scripture:

"Do you not know that your bodies are temples of the Holy Spirit…?"
1 Corinthians 6:19, NIV

Real-Life Story:

When Frank entered the early days of grief, he couldn't sleep and began losing weight. His heart would race for no clear reason. A counselor helped him realize his grief wasn't just emotional—it was physical. Naming that gave him permission to rest and care for his body, even if the pain hadn't fully lifted.

Fred noticed that during intense grief, his sleep patterns were off, his appetite changed, and he felt physically drained. He wasn't "just sad"—his body was calling a timeout, too.

Common Physical Symptoms of Grief:

- Fatigue or insomnia

- Sleep disruption (too much or too little)

- Headaches

- Digestive issues

- Muscle tension

- Brain fog

- Immune suppression

- Appetite changes

"Grief is a full-contact experience. You don't just feel it in your heart—you carry it in your shoulders, your stomach, your spine."
– Grief is a Team Sport

Reflection Questions:

1. How has your body reacted to your grief?

_____

_____

_____

_____

2. Are you giving your body space to heal—or pushing through the pain?

_____

_____

_____

_____

3. What small act of care can you offer your body today?

_____

_____

_____

_____

Activity: Your Self-Care Game Plan

Rate your current habits on a scale of 1 to 5 (1 = poor, 5 = excellent):

Area	Rating	One thing I can do to improve
Drink Water		
Eat Good Nutrition		
Exercise/Movement		

List 3 small things you can do this week to support your physical healing:

1._____

2._____

3._____

Prayer Prompt:

Dear God,

Help me listen to my body. I've been through so much. Teach me to rest, to move with intention, and to honor this temple You've given me. Amen.

Closing Thought:

You can't outplay your pain. Every athlete needs recovery time. Let your body grieve. Let it rest. Let it be part of the team that leads you to healing.

GRIEF IS A COLLECTIVE
JOURNEY, BUT THE MOST
CRUCIAL PLAYER IS THE
INNER VOICE.

Chapter 7:

LOCKER ROOM TALK – THE POWER OF WORDS IN GRIEF

Objective:

To recognize how words—both internal and external—can either wound or heal, and to equip you to speak truth and compassion to yourself and others in grief.

Key Scripture:

"The tongue has the power of life and death…"
Proverbs 18:21, NIV

Real-Life Story:

At his brother's funeral, Mark heard well-meaning comments like "He's in a better place" and "Everything happens for a reason." But those words didn't bring comfort. What did help was when someone simply said, "I'm here. I don't have words, but I love you." In the locker room of grief, we learn the power—and limits—of language.

After his brother's death, Barry was told, "At least he's in a better place." Though well-meaning, those words felt hollow and rushed. But a teammate in grief simply said, "I'm here. No words, just presence." That changed everything.

The Words We Hear (and Say):

Like a coach's halftime speech, words can reframe the moment—or reinforce the pain.

- **Harmful Words:** "It was God's will." "Be strong." "You should be over it."

- "At least they're no longer suffering."

- "God needed another angel."

- "You need to be strong."

- "You should be over it by now."

- "Don't cry."

Reflection Prompt:

Have you received any of these comments? How did they make you feel?

- **Healing Words:** "This is hard, and I'm here." "You're not alone." "You don't have to pretend."

- "I don't know what to say, but I'm here."

- "This must be incredibly hard for you."

- "Tell me about them—I'd love to know more."

- "You're not alone."

- "I'm praying for strength and comfort for you."

> *"Some words bring water to dry ground. Others just stir the dust. Speak life."*
> *– Grief is a Team Sport*

Fill-in-the-Blank Activity:

- A phrase I wish someone had said to me is: _____.

- A phrase I wish people would stop saying is: _____.

- When I talk to myself about my grief, I often say: _____.

Activity: Rewriting the Script

Choose one unhelpful phrase you've heard and rewrite it into a life-giving one.

Example:

Instead of: "You'll get over it."
Try: "This won't always hurt this way—but your love will always remain."

Reflection Questions:

1. What words have helped you in your grief?

_____

_____

_____

_____

2. What words have hurt or shut you down?

_____

_____

_____

_____

3. What would you say to someone grieving, knowing what you know now?

_____

_____

_____

_____

Closing Thought:

Words are locker room fuel. Speak life to yourself and others. Let your language become part of the healing game plan.

JUST AS NO PLAYER CAN WIN A
GAME SINGLE-HANDEDLY, NO
ONE SHOULD BE EXPECTED TO
OVERCOME GRIEF WITHOUT
SUPPORT.

Chapter 8:

WHEN GRIEF GETS COMPLICATED

Objective:

To understand complicated grief, recognize its signs, and embrace tools and support systems for healing.

Key Scripture:

"Come to me, all you who are weary and burdened, and I will give you rest."

Matthew 11:28, NIV

Real-Life Story:

After months of functioning "normally" at work, Fred noticed he still couldn't sleep and had trouble concentrating. What felt like normal grief had turned into prolonged sorrow. It wasn't just sadness—it was stuckness. He realized he needed more than prayer; he needed a grief counselor. That decision marked the beginning of a deeper level of healing.

Dr. Michaels met someone whose father had died twenty years earlier, but she still couldn't walk past his photo without falling apart. She wasn't "stuck"—she was silently suffering with complicated grief and had never been invited to get help.

What Is Complicated Grief?

Complicated grief (also called Prolonged Grief Disorder) is when intense grief lasts longer than expected and interferes with daily functioning. Grief becomes complicated when it:

- Lingers intensely beyond six months to a year
- Disrupts daily function
- Feels like despair with no relief
- Involves trauma, regret, or unresolved relationships

Warning Signs of Complicated Grief:

- Avoidance of reminders

- Numbness or detachment

- Ongoing guilt or blame

- Depression or suicidal thoughts

- Substance abuse or unhealthy coping

Quote to Reflect On:

"Healing doesn't mean the damage never existed. It means the damage no longer controls your life." – Akshay Dubey

1. Do any of these signs sound familiar to you or someone you know?

2. Have you ever been afraid to ask for help? Why?

Important Note:

Complicated grief is not a failure of faith. It's a call for deeper care.

Activity: The Help Roster

Make a list of people or professionals you could call on when grief gets too heavy:

- _____ (Friend)

- _____ (Therapist/Counselor)

- _____ (Pastor)

- _____ (Support Group)

"When grief becomes an injury instead of just a wound, it's time for a different kind of team— counselors, pastors, clinicians. Healing needs a game plan." – Grief is a Team Sport

Think of 2-3 people or resources you could reach out to this week:

Resource/Person	Contact Info or Step to Take
Ex: Christian counselor	www.griefshare.org or a local therapist
Trusted friend or family	
Faith leader or support group	

Prayer Prompt:

Dear God,

Sometimes this pain feels too deep. If I need more help, give me the courage to ask. Send the right teammates at the right time. Amen.

Closing Thought:

Complicated grief needs a care team. It doesn't mean you're weak—it means you're worth healing.

DEALING WITH
NON-DEATH LOSSES
REQUIRES INTENTIONAL
STRATEGIES.

Chapter 9

INVISIBLE GRIEF – THE LOSSES PEOPLE DON'T SEE

Objective:

To validate non-death grief experiences and encourage honest processing of losses that others may overlook.

Key Scripture:

"There is a time for everything... a time to mourn and a time to dance."

Ecclesiastes 3:1a, 4b, NIV

Real-Life Story:

Denise experienced deep sorrow after an unexpected job loss. Though no one had died, she grieved the loss of identity, routine, and purpose. Others didn't understand why she was so upset. That's when she realized: not all grief wears black.

Derek once counseled a woman who was grieving the loss of her independence after a car accident, but everyone around her said, "At least you're alive." She didn't feel seen—until someone acknowledged her invisible grief.

Types of Invisible Grief:

- Divorce or relationship breakup
- Loss of health or ability
- Job loss or retirement
- Miscarriage or infertility

- Estrangement or emotional abandonment
- Loss of identity or dreams

"Just because the world doesn't send flowers doesn't mean your loss isn't real. Some grief lives in quiet corners—and needs gentle light to heal." – Grief is a Team Sport

Reflection Questions:

1. What invisible losses have you experienced?

_____

_____

_____

_____

2. Have others minimized or misunderstood your pain?

_____

_____

_____

_____

3. How can you give yourself permission to grieve?

_____

_____

_____

_____

Fill-in-the-Blank Activity:

- I grieved silently when _____.

- I wish people knew that even though it wasn't a death, it still hurt because _____.

- I need to give myself permission to feel _____.

Activity: Honoring My Invisible Loss

Write a letter or journal entry to yourself naming and validating a non-death loss. End with a phrase like: "You mattered. That season mattered. I give myself permission to grieve it."

Prayer Prompt:

Dear God,

Thank You for seeing the grief no one else sees. Help me honor the quiet pain and trust that You collect every tear—even the invisible ones. Amen.

Closing Thought:

Invisible grief still counts. It may not make headlines, but it's written on your heart. And God reads every word.

GRIEF IS A TEAM SPORT—AND
NO ONE HEALS FROM LOSS BY
SITTING ON THE SIDELINES.

Chapter 10:

TEAMWORK MAKES HEALING WORK

Objective:

To reinforce the concept that healing is not a solo sport—grief recovery thrives in community.

Key Scripture:

"Carry each other's burdens, and in this way you will fulfill the law of Christ."

Galatians 6:2, NIV

Real-Life Story:

After his brother's funeral, Felix didn't realize how much he needed a team until others showed up with food, rides, prayers, and just silent company. Healing began not when he stood alone—but when he let others into the process.

The Team Sport Mindset of Healing:

- **Lifters/Coaches** – Mentors, pastors, therapists

- **Listeners/Teammates** – Friends, family, grief groups

- **Weepers/Trainers** – Those who give you space and don't rush the process

- **Supporters/Fans in the Stands** – People who cheer you on from far and near

- **You** – You are still on the team. Show up.

"People may not remember what you said, but they will always remember how you made them feel" – Maya Angelou

Reflection Questions:

1. Who are your teammates in grief?

_____

_____

_____

_____

2. Where do you need more support?

_____

_____

_____

_____

3. Who might need *you* on their healing team?

_____

_____

_____

_____

Activity: Build Your Healing Roster

Create your grief recovery team chart:

Role	Name/Contact
Lifter/Coach	_____
Listener/Teammate	_____
Weeper/Trainer	_____
Support/Fan in the Stands	_____

Prayer Prompt:

Dear God,

I don't want to grieve alone. Thank You for my team. Show me how to give and receive help. Strengthen us all. Amen.

Closing Thought:

Grief is a chapter—not the whole story. You're still here. You're still healing. And there is hope ahead.

Healing is teamwork. The team may change. The pace may shift. But the goal is the same: wholeness, one play at a time.

Hello

I'm Dr. Fred Batten, Jr.

Speaker • Author • Leader • Pastor • Chaplain

Empowering individuals to navigate grief, push past the pain, and forge a new path forward.

ABOUT

- 25+ Years of Leadership Experience: With a strong background in guiding organizations, communities, and individuals through challenging transitions.
- Expert in Grief & Loss: Certified in leadership by the John Maxwell Team, Dr. Batten specializes in helping people cope with loss, find hope, and rebuild resiliently.
- Pastor & Chaplain: Bringing compassionate insight to every stage of the healing journey, blending empathy with practical strategies.
- Author: His book, Wisdom from Generation to Generation, offers timeless insights and and actionable advice for thriving across life's seasons.

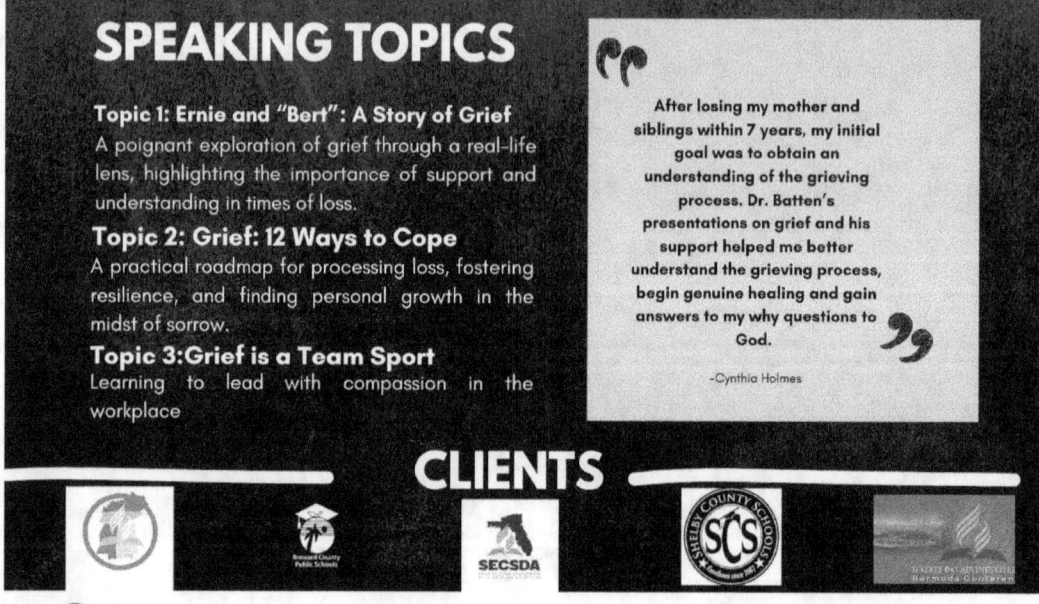

SPEAKING TOPICS

Topic 1: Ernie and "Bert": A Story of Grief
A poignant exploration of grief through a real-life lens, highlighting the importance of support and understanding in times of loss.

Topic 2: Grief: 12 Ways to Cope
A practical roadmap for processing loss, fostering resilience, and finding personal growth in the midst of sorrow.

Topic 3: Grief is a Team Sport
Learning to lead with compassion in the workplace

> After losing my mother and siblings within 7 years, my initial goal was to obtain an understanding of the grieving process. Dr. Batten's presentations on grief and his support helped me better understand the grieving process, begin genuine healing and gain answers to my why questions to God.
>
> -Cynthia Holmes

CLIENTS

901-552-8482   drfbattenjr@gmail.com   fbattenjr.com

Purchase the *Grief is a Team Sport* book to use
as a companion with this workbook.

Available in Paperback.

ISBN: ISBN: 978-1-964972-15-2

www.ingramcontent.com/pod-product-compliance
Lightning Source LLC
Chambersburg PA
CBHW081541120626
46550CB00009B/2821